First published in Great Britain in 2006 by HarperCollins Children's Books.
HarperCollins Children's Books is a division of HarperCollins Publishers Ltd.
The HarperCollins Children's Books website is www.harpercollinschildrensbooks.co.uk
1 3 5 7 9 10 8 6 4 2
© The Football Association Limited 2006
Photography © Empics/PA 2006
Writers: Lindsey Kelk and Paul Wray
The FA Crest and The FA England Crest are official trade marks of The Football Association Limited
and are the subject of extensive trade mark registrations worldwide.
Produced by HarperCollins under licence by the Football Association Limited.

TheFA.com

All information correct at time of printing, April 2006
ISBN-13: 978-0-00-721699-4
ISBN: 0-00-721699-8
A CIP catalogue for this title is available from the British Library. All rights reserved.

THE OFFICIAL ENGLAND ANNUAL 2007

HarperCollins *Children's Books*

World Cup years are always exciting and 2006 was no exception.

A dramatic quarter-final exit to Portugal on penalties, the saga of Wayne Rooney's race to be fit for Germany, a tearful David Beckham quitting as captain and the end of Sven-Goran Eriksson's reign as England boss. It has been a memorable year for the Three Lions.

Looking ahead, England are now aiming for qualification for Euro 2008 in Austria and Switzerland under a new manager, Steve McClaren.

This annual is crammed with facts, stats, activities and player tips to keep you going until Euro 2008. Discover everything about your favourite England player, and there's also advice on how to improve your own game.

So enjoy The Official England Annual 2007 and another action-packed year following the England team.

Enjoyed Germany 2006?

Facts and stats of all the World Cup action.

- A total of 12 stadiums were used to host 64 games of the 2006 World Cup in Germany. The opening match took place in the new 66,000-capacity Stadion München in Munich on 9 June.

- The 2006 World Cup final took place in Berlin's Olympiastadion in front of 69,000 people on 9 July.

- Berlin's Olympiastadion was originally built for the 1936 Olympics which famously saw US sprinter Jesse Owens win four gold medals. For the 2006 World Cup, it's had a £160m face lift.

- The brand-new £186m stadium in Munich has a very futuristic design. The outside has a translucent, diamond-shaped shell, which acts as a projection surface so the stadium can have a kaleidoscope of colours projected onto it!

- As well as Munich and Berlin – Cologne, Dortmund, Frankfurt, Gelsenkirchen, Hamburg, Hannover, Kaiserslautern, Leipzig, Nuremberg and Stuttgart also hosted World Cup matches.

- The official mascots of the 2006 World Cup – Goleo VI the lion and his pal Pille the ball – were created by the Jim Henson Company who are famous for making The Muppets and Sesame Street.

- The whole world watched the World Cup! It's estimated that an accumulated TV audience of 32 billion people tuned in to the 64 matches of Germany 2006.

- For the Brazil v Germany 2002 World Cup final, one billion people across the world watched it on TV.

- Wayne Rooney is only the third English player to see red in the World Cup finals when he was sent off against Portugal. Ray Wilkins was dismissed during the 1986 World Cup in Mexico and David Beckham met a similar fate against Argentina during the 1998 tournament in France.

- David Beckham's 60th minute free-kick against Ecuador saw him become England's first player to score in three World Cups.

- Brazil's Ronaldo became the highest scorer in World Cup finals history with his goal against Ghana during the 2006 World Cup. He has a tally of 15 goals.

- France's defeat of Brazil in the quarter-finals ended an 11-game winning streak – a World Cup finals record.

- Steve McClaren is England's 14th manager, including caretakers, since the second world war.

World Cup winners		Most World Cups	
1930	Uruguay	5	Brazil
1934	Italy	4	Italy
1938	Italy	3	Germany/ West Germany
1950	Uruguay	2	Uruguay & Argentina
1954	West Germany	1	England & France
1958	Brazil		
1962	Brazil		
1966	England		
1970	Brazil		
1974	West Germany		
1978	Argentina		
1982	Italy		
1986	Argentina		
1990	West Germany		
1994	Brazil		
1998	France		
2002	Brazil		
2006	Italy		

Michael Owen

Name: Michael Owen

DOB: 14.12.79

Club: Newcastle United

England Debut:
England vs. Chile 02.98

Position in England Team:
Forward

Caps: 80

Goals: 36

Biography
A knee injury just a minute into the group match against Sweden cruelly cut short Michael Owen's 2006 World Cup. He is third on England's all-time goal-scorers' list and the world-class marksman is best remembered for his solo goal against Argentina in the 1998 World Cup and his hat-trick against Germany in 2001.

England & Newcastle Utd

Frank Lampard

Name: Frank Lampard

DOB: 20.06.78

Club: Chelsea

England Debut:
England vs. Belgium 10.99

Position in England Team:
Midfielder

Caps: 45

Goals: 11

Biography

Frank is a tireless runner and crucial goal-scorer from midfield for both club and country. The Chelsea player was a star performer for England in Euro 2004 finding the net three times and the 28-year-old was unlucky not to add to his tally in the 2006 World Cup as he was a constant threat in the box.

Rio Ferdinand

Name: Rio Ferdinand

DOB: 07.11.78

Club: Manchester United

England Debut:
England vs. Cameroon 11.97

Position in England Team:
Defender

Caps: 52

Goals: 1

Biography
A pacy, ball-playing centre-back, Rio was an ever-present in defence for England during the 2006 World Cup. He started his career at West Ham United before moving from Leeds United to Manchester United for £29.1m in July 2002. Rio's only goal was scored against Denmark in the 2002 World Cup.

England & Man United

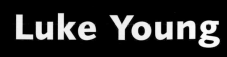

Luke Young

Name: Luke Young

DOB: 19.07.1979

Club: Charlton Athletic

England Debut:
England vs. USA, 05.05

Position in England Team:
Defender

Caps: 7

Goals: 0

Biography
Luke started his career as a trainee at Tottenham where he spent four seasons, making 58 League appearances before moving south of the river to The Valley in 2001. Young has a wealth of U18 and U21 England team experience to bring to the senior team.

England & Charlton Athletic (13)

Jermain Defoe

Name: Jermain Defoe

DOB: 07.10.82

Club: Tottenham Hotspur

England Debut:
England vs. Sweden 03.04

Position in England Team:
Forward

Caps: 16

Goals: 1

Biography
Defoe is one of England's most exciting young prospects. After being linked to both Manchester United and Arsenal, he finally put pen to paper with Spurs to return to the Premiership in January 2004.

England & Tottenham

Name: Ashley Cole

DOB: 20.12.80

Club: Arsenal

England Debut:
England vs. Albania 03.01

Position in England Team:
Defender

Caps: 51

Goals: 0

Biography
Regarded as one of the world's best left-backs, Ashley has missed just 17 minutes of England's 2006 World Cup, Euro 2004 and 2002 World Cup campaigns.
Expect the 25-year-old to continue to be a vital player for his country as his attacking instincts and tigerish defence make him invaluable.

Wes Brown

Name: Wes Brown

DOB: 13.10.79

Club: Manchester United

England Debut:
England vs. Hungary 04.99

Position in England Team:
Defender

Caps: 9

Goals: 0

Biography
An accomplished central defender with a gift for reading the game, Brown was in fine form as he returned to the England starting line-up for 2005's February friendly with Holland. The Manchester-born defender's career breakthrough came during the 1998-99 season as he first gained a regular place in Sir Alex Ferguson's defence and then made his full England debut against Hungary in Budapest.

England & Man United

Steven Gerrard

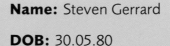

Name: Steven Gerrard

DOB: 30.05.80

Club: Liverpool

England Debut:
England vs. Ukraine 05.00

Position in England Team:
Midfielder

Caps: 47

Goals: 9

Biography

The Liverpool captain crowned an amazing 2005-06 season with two goals for his country during the World Cup in Germany. A complete midfielder who can pass, tackle and shoot, Steven scored a memorable last-minute equaliser in the 2006 FA Cup final to help his beloved Reds to victory against West Ham United.

David James

Name: David James

DOB: 01.08.70

Club: Manchester City

England Debut:
England vs. Mexico 03.97

Position in England Team:
Goalkeeper

Caps: 34

Goals: 0

Biography
England's second choice keeper, David James is an athletic shot-stopper who is a consistent Premiership performer for Manchester City. He was between the sticks for his country during Euro 2004 before Paul Robinson claimed the No 1 jersey in September 2004.

England & Man City

Jermaine Jenas

Name: Jermaine Jenas

DOB: 18.02.83

Club: Tottenham Hotspur

England Debut:
England vs. Australia 02.03

Position in England Team:
Midfielder

Caps: 15

Goals: 0

Biography
A £7m move from Newcastle United to Tottenham in August 2005 re-ignited Jermaine's England prospects with an impressive season in the Spurs midfield. An unused member of the 2006 World Cup squad, expect the strong-running 23-year-old to feature more and more for the Three Lions.

Copy and Colour

Goalkeeper

The goalkeeper is one of the most important members of a team. It's not just keeping out the ball, you have to communicate with your defenders all the time.

But of course, the goalie always has to be prepared for a shot, which can be really tricky if nothing happens at his end of the pitch for ages!

- Try and line your body up to where the ball is on the pitch, especially if it is coming at you.

- Once someone shoots for goal, try and wrap your arms around the ball and pull it towards your stomach.

- Let your body go floppy so the ball doesn't hurt you in case the opposition kicked it hard.

- As you straighten up hold the ball tight to your chest and don't let it go.

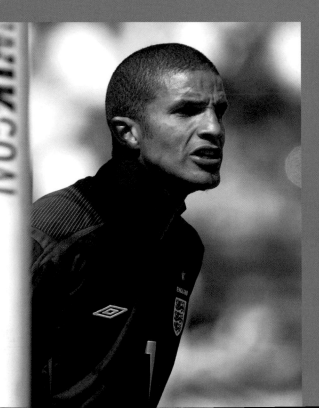

Midfielders do a lot of running up and down the field and are sometimes responsible for taking penalties, like David Beckham.

Taking the perfect penalty isn't easy but if you follow these tips, you should hit your target.

- **Take four steps back from the penalty spot.**

- **It's best to decide where to hit the ball before you run up to it! Are you going to kick it as hard as you can and hope the goalie can't catch it or try and place the ball out of the goalie's reach?**

- **Some players imagine there is a big target in the goal and try to hit it to help them kick the ball into the right place.**

- **The most important thing you can do is practise, practise and practise!**

Using your head

- It's not just about hitting things with your feet – all the best footballers use their heads as well!

- It helps to be taller when going for a header but a great jump will give you just as much height – don't forget to practise.

- Heading the ball is simple enough, just get high and be brave BUT always be safe – avoid head-to-head clashes with other players.

- It might sound silly to read but the hardest and most important part of taking a header, is keeping your eyes open.

Passing

Passing is also really important. It might seem basic but if you can't pass, you can't play!

- If you're right-footed, put your left foot out to one side of the ball and kick. Left-footed players should use their right foot.

- Try and hit the centre of the ball with your foot instead of the sides – this should keep it low and easier to control.

- Balance yourself with your arms and keep your eyes on the ball.

Tackling

Tackling can be a risky business. If you're not aggressive enough, your opponent will get by. Too aggressive and you'll get sent off!

Here's how to execute the perfect tackle:

• Get in front of your opponent quickly but don't go for the ball too early or they will just whizz around you.

• Stand your ground and wait for the best time to make a challenge. Sometimes just putting your opponent under pressure will cause them to make a mistake.

• When you think you can win the ball your weight should be moving forward as you prepare to tackle. Use the inside of your foot just as your opponent looks to make a move.

• If the ball gets stuck between yours or your opponent's feet, use the top of your foot to try and lift it away.

• Make sure you keep your ankle and leg firm throughout making a tackle – you are less likely to get injured if you are committed to the challenge.

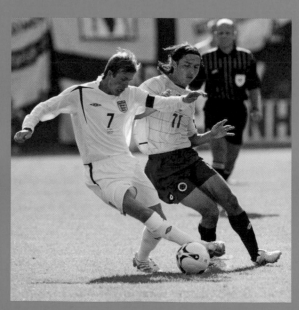

Scoring Goals!

The strikers job is to score goals — and lots of them. The midfielders and defenders will be constantly feeding through balls and the striker needs to be completely aware of everything that's happening on the pitch.

- Accuracy is just as important as power when going for a goal. Making sure you hit the opposite corner of the goal to where the goalkeeper is standing will give you a better chance of scoring.

- Try and disguise where you're going to shoot, it will really throw the defenders and goalkeepers off.

- If you can look into one corner and strike the ball at the other you've a great chance of fooling the keeper.

- It's not just about getting your head down and pegging the ball with your foot. A great striker uses their whole body to score the best goals.

- Your standing foot shouldn't be too near the ball, but it needs to be close enough to help you balance.

- It's also really important to keep the ball down. Make sure you've got your body over the ball and strike the centre of the ball, not the edges.

- Shooting is a hard skill to learn and there's a lot to remember. The key is to practise as much as possible and hopefully you'll soon be scoring for England!

Taking a Corner

Taking a corner is very difficult. Follow these tips and always get your corner kicks in the area:

- Place the ball in the corner area.

- Run up to the ball and kick it towards the goal area.

- To curve the ball from right to left, use the inside of your right foot, hitting the bottom half of the right side of the ball.

- If you want to curve the ball from left to right, use the outside of your right foot and aim to make contact with the bottom half of the left side of the ball.

- Don't kick the ball too hard. It's more important to hit it on target!

David Beckham

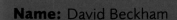

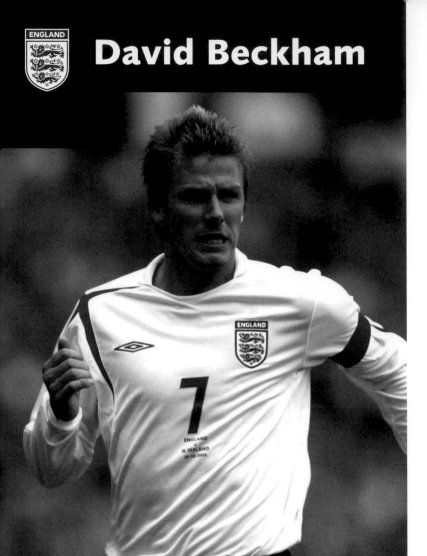

Name: David Beckham

DOB: 02.05.75

Club: Real Madrid

England Debut:
England vs. Moldova 09.96

Position in England Team:
Midfielder

Caps: 94

Goals: 17

Biography:
Following England's World Cup exit, a tearful David gave up the captain's armband after 58 games but his influence remains as he approaches 100 caps for his country. "Becks" is still a world-class crosser of the ball and a deadly free-kick specialist as his stunning winner against Ecuador demonstrated in Germany.

England & Real Madrid

Wayne Rooney

Name: Wayne Rooney

DOB: 24.10.85

Club: Manchester United

England Debut:
England vs. Australia 02.03

Position in England Team:
Forward

Caps: 33

Goals: 11

Biography

Whether Wayne's foot would heal in time for the 2006 World Cup became a national obsession and England's premier striker did return, making four appearances. A red card in the quarter-final shattered his World Cup dreams but the 20-year-old is sure to prove himself to be one of the world's best football talents in the coming years.

John Terry

Name: John Terry

DOB: 07.12.80

Club: Chelsea

England Debut:
England vs. Serbia & Montenegro 06.03

Position in England Team:
Defender

Caps: 29

Goals: 1

Biography
A natural leader, the Chelsea captain is a commanding presence at centre-back for his country and he's also useful at set-pieces. John showed this lionhearted, never-say-die attitude when England were down to 10 men for nearly an hour against Portugal in the World Cup quarter-final.

England & Chelsea

Gary Neville

Name: Gary Neville

DOB: 18.02.75

Club: Manchester United

England Debut:
England vs. Japan 06.95

Position in England Team:
Defender

Caps: 81

Goals: 0

Biography
Gary is an unsung hero for England and has been his country's first choice right-back for more than 10 years. He is also the most experienced major tournament campaigner, having played in Euro 1996, 1998 World Cup, Euro 2000, Euro 2004 and 2006 World Cup.

Jamie Carragher

Name: Jamie Carragher

DOB: 28.01.78

Club: Liverpool

England Debut:
England vs. Hungary 04.99

Position in England Team:
Defender

Caps: 29

Goals: 0

Biography
Liverpool-born Jamie is a versatile man-marker who can play at centre-back or right-back and his whole-hearted performances were key to the Reds' 2005 European Cup success. A strong character who'll no doubt bounce back from his penalty shoot-out miss against Portugal in the World Cup quarter-final.

England & Liverpool

Michael Carrick

Name: Michael Carrick

DOB: 28.07.81

Club: Tottenham Hotspur

England Debut:
England vs. Mexico 05.01

Position in England Team:
Midfielder

Caps: 7

Goals: 0

Biography

Injuries have limited Michael Carrick's England caps but his ball-passing abilities are slowly being shown on the international stage. The Spurs midfielder produced a controlled performance against Ecuador in the 2006 World Cup and, at 25 years old, Michael still has time to turn his promise as a youngster into regular performances for England.

Peter Crouch

Name: Peter Crouch

DOB: 30.01.81

Club: Liverpool

England Debut:
England vs. Colombia 05.05

Position in England Team:
Striker

Caps: 11

Goals: 6

Biography
The 2.04m-tall striker is too easily dismissed as a lanky target man despite great ball control. The £7m Liverpool player scored six goals in five games for England, including a vital 83rd-minute opener against Trinidad & Tobago during the World Cup, which should finally give him the confidence on the international stage.

England & Liverpool

Shaun Wright-Philips

Name: Shaun Wright-Phillips

DOB: 25.10.81

Club: Chelsea

England Debut:
England vs. Ukraine 08.04

Position in England Team:
Midfielder

Caps: 8

Goals: 1

Biography
Wright-Phillips enjoyed a great season with Manchester City in 2003-04 and earned his first call-up to the Senior squad to face Sweden but never made it on to the pitch. Starting where he left off, Wright-Phillips made his debut as a substitute in a friendly with Ukraine in August 2004. Not content with the new cap alone, he also produced a fine goal to help England round off a 3-0 win.

England & Chelsea

Paul Robinson

Name: Paul Robinson

DOB: 15.10.79

Club: Tottenham Hotspur

England Debut:
England vs. Australia 02.03

Position in England Team:
Goalkeeper

Caps: 26

Goals: 0

Biography
Paul established himself as England's No 1 keeper in September 2004 against Poland and has never looked back. Still only 26, his consistent and commanding presence between the posts should see the Spurs star the first choice for many years to come. He was ever-present during the 2006 World Cup, making five appearances.

ENGLAND

England & Tottenham

We've got the inside information on all your favourite players!

What's your favourite... Game?

Beckham:	Pac Man
Bridge:	Monopoly/Pro-Evolution Soccer
Carragher:	Pac Man
Carrick:	Pro-Evolution Soccer
A Cole:	Monopoly/Pro-Evolution Soccer
J Cole:	Pro-Evolution Soccer
Crouch:	Tiger Woods PSP
Defoe:	Pro-Evolution Soccer
Gerrard:	Tiger Woods PSP
James:	Ridge Racer PSP
King:	Pro-Evolution Soccer
Lampard:	Monopoly
G Neville:	Monopoly
P Neville:	Balderdash
Owen:	Monopoly
Terry:	Pro-Evolution Soccer
Wright-Phillips:	Snakes & Ladders

What's your favourite... Car?

Beckham:	Range Rover
Bridge:	Porsche 911 Turbo
Carragher:	Range Rover
Carrick:	Mercedes SLR
A Cole:	Aston Martin
J Cole:	Ferrari
Crouch:	BMW X5
Defoe:	Range Rover
Gerrard:	Bentley GT Continental
James:	Ford Escort Van MkII
King:	Bentley GT
Lampard:	Aston Martin
G Neville:	Bentley GT
P Neville:	Mini
Owen:	Jaguar
Terry:	Bentley GT
Wright-Phillips:	Aston Martin

Footballers' Favourites

What's your favourite... Music?

Beckham:	Hip hop
Bridge:	Bob Marley
Carragher:	Oasis
Carrick:	Usher
A Cole:	R&B
J Cole:	Oasis
Crouch:	U2
Defoe:	R&B
Gerrard:	Dance
James:	Hip Hop/Funk
Lampard:	R&B
G Neville:	Rock
P Neville:	Usher
Owen:	Chart music
Terry:	R&B
Wright-Phillips:	R&B

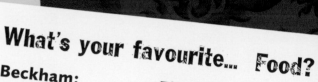

What's your favourite... Food?

Beckham:	Pie & mash
Bridge:	Pasta
Carragher:	Lasagne
Carrick:	Italian
A Cole:	Nando's
J Cole:	Mum's Roast Dinner
Crouch:	Roast beef and Yorkshire puddings
Defoe:	Mum's West Indian foo
Gerrard:	Chinese/Italian
James:	Chicken
King:	Italian
Lampard:	Pasta
G Neville:	English
P Neville:	Pasta
Owen:	Spanish Tapas
Terry:	Chicken & pasta
Wright-Phillips:	Chinese

What's your favourite... Film?

Beckham:	Last Samurai
Bridge:	Goodfellas
Carragher:	One Flew Over the Cuckoo's Nest
Carrick:	The Usual Suspects
A Cole:	The Negotiator
J Cole:	Escape to Victory
Crouch:	Seven
Defoe:	Rocky IV
Gerrard:	Scarface
James:	Too many to pick one!
King:	Scarface
Lampard:	Gladiator
G Neville:	Braveheart
P Neville:	Man on Fire
Owen:	Ocean's Eleven
Terry:	Happy Gilmour
Wright-Phillips:	Scarface

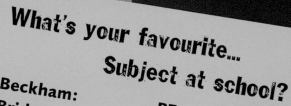

What's your favourite... Subject at school?

Beckham:	PE
Bridge:	PE
Carragher:	PE
Carrick:	PE
A Cole:	PE
Crouch:	English
Defoe:	PE
Gerrard:	PE
James:	PE
King:	PE
Lampard:	History
G Neville:	Maths
P Neville:	Geography
Owen:	Geography
Terry:	PE
Wright-Phillips:	PE

Footballers' Favourites

What's your favourite... TV show?

Beckham:	Only Fools and Horses
Bridge:	24
Carragher:	Match of the Day
Carrick:	24
A Cole:	Coronation Street
J Cole:	Friends
Crouch:	24
Defoe:	Big Brother
Gerrard:	The Office
James:	The Bear in the Big Blue House
King:	24
Lampard:	The Sopranos
G Neville:	24
P Neville:	Friends
Owen:	The Office
Terry:	Only Fools and Horses
Wright-Phillips:	Only Fools and Horses

What's your favourite... Sport apart from football?

Bridge:	Athletics
Carragher:	Boxing
Carrick:	Formula1
A Cole:	Golf
J Cole:	Boxing
Crouch:	Tennis
Defoe:	Basketball
Gerrard:	Golf
James:	American Football
King:	Basketball
Lampard:	Cricket
G Neville:	Golf/Cricket
P Neville:	Cricket
Owen:	Racing/Golf
Terry:	Golf
Wright-Phillips:	Tennis

What's your favourite...
Pizza topping?

Beckham:	Ham & mushroom
Bridge:	Pepperoni
Carragher:	Meat feast
Carrick:	Seafood
A Cole:	Spicy Chicken
J Cole:	Garlic
Crouch:	Beef
Defoe:	Chicken with extra cheese
Gerrard:	Mozzerella
James:	Chicken
King:	Pepperoni
Lampard:	Everything but anchovies
G Neville:	Ham, mushrooms & onions
P Neville:	Ham & mushrooms
Owen:	Chicken & pineapple
Terry:	American
Wright-Phillips:	Meat & chillies

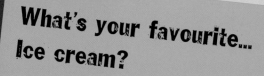

What's your favourite...
Ice cream?

Beckham:	Cookies & cream
Bridge:	Chocolate
Carragher:	Vanilla
Carrick:	Mint Choc Chip
A Cole:	Chocolate
J Cole:	Vanilla
Crouch:	Vanilla
Defoe:	Vanilla
Gerrard:	Vanilla
King:	Vanilla
Lampard:	Vanilla
G Neville:	Vanilla
P Neville:	Toffee
Owen:	Vanilla
Terry:	Coconut
Wright-Phillips:	Banana
	Chocolate

Footballers' Favourites

Who is your favourite footballing idol?

Beckham: Bryan Robson - he wore no. 7 for United and England

Bridge: Matt Le Tissier - I was a big Southampton fan as a kid

Carragher: Kenny Dalglish - great player and manager

Carrick: Paul Gascoigne - he's a legend

A Cole: Roberto Carlos - I love the way he plays and I'd like to play like him

J Cole: Paul Gascoigne - absolutely brilliant skills

Crouch: Gianluca Vialli - I was a big fan of Italian football as a kid

Defoe: Ian Wright - he played with so much style and charisma

Gerrard: Kenny Dalglish - best LFC player ever!!!

James: Michael Owen - top bloke

King: Maldini - everything I hope to be

Lampard: Paul Gascoigne

G Neville: Bryan Robson - supported United growing up

P Neville: Bryan Robson - gave everything for club and country

Owen: Gary Lineker - scored lots of goals

Terry: Tony Adams - love the way he played

Wright-Phillips: Ian Wright

What was the best moment of your career?

Beckham:	**Winning the treble at Man Utd in 1999**
Bridge:	**Scoring at Arsenal in Champions League QF 2004 and winning Premier League**
Carragher:	**Champions League Final 2005**
Carrick:	**Making full England debut vs USA**
A Cole:	**Winning the Premiership twice**
J Cole:	**Winning the League**
Crouch:	**Making my debut for England**
Defoe:	**Scoring for England on my first start**
Gerrard:	**Lifting the Champions League trophy**
James:	**My England debut**
King:	**Scoring on my full debut for England v Portugal**
Lampard:	**Winning the Premiership**
G Neville:	**European Cup win**
P Neville:	**First time I played for United**
Owen:	**FA Cup Final**
Terry:	**Winning the Premiership**
Wright-Phillips:	**First being selected and then scoring on my England debut**

What's the funniest thing that's happened in your footballing career?

Beckham:	**Playing at Wembley and then realising my shirt name was spelt incorrectly!**
Carragher:	**Putting the captain's armband on for England!**
Carrick:	**FA Youth Cup vs Walsall - we scored and celebrated by having a team photo taken by the corner flag!**
J Cole:	**I enjoy every minute - it's all great fun.**
Crouch:	**When I was at Portsmouth, I tried a double step-over in front of the away fans...I trod on the ball and fell over!**
Gerrard:	**Too many to say one!**
Owen:	**Streaker on full debut!**

Describe yourself in three words?

Beckham:	Committed, honest, hard-working
Bridge:	Generous, thoughtful, determined
Carragher:	Likes a laugh!
Carrick:	Kind and generous!
A Cole:	Kind, outgoing, friendly
J Cole:	Contented, happy, motivated
Crouch:	Fun, determined, ambitious
Defoe:	Funny, ambitious, honest
Gerrard:	Ambitious, generous, dedicated
James:	Happy being me
King:	Kind, determined, ambitious
Lampard:	Kind, generous, friendly
P Neville:	Happy, calm, hard-working
Terry:	Determined, proud, loyal
Wright-Phillips:	Hyperactive, small, dedicated

What would you be if you weren't a footballer?

Bridge:	PE Teacher
Carragher:	Football Manager
Carrick:	Sports Coach or Teacher
A Cole:	Lifeguard
Crouch:	Tennis Player
Defoe:	A dancer
Gerrard:	Professional Golfer
James:	Charity Worker
King:	Football Agent
Lampard:	Lawyer
P Neville:	Cricketer
Owen:	Golfer
Terry:	Golfer

Who is the practical joker of the squad?

Beckham: Wayne Rooney
Bridge: David James
Carragher: Wayne Rooney
J Cole: Wayne Rooney/Rio Ferdinand
Crouch: David James
Defoe: Rio Ferdinand
Gerrard: Wayne Rooney
King: David James
Lampard: Wayne Rooney
P Neville: Wayne Rooney
Owen: Jamie Carragher
Terry: Wayne Rooney

Who is the brainiest member of the squad?

Beckham: Gary Neville / David James
Bridge: David James
Carragher: Gary Neville
A Cole: David James
Crouch: David James
Defoe: Robert Green
James: Frank Lampard
King: Ashley Cole
Lampard: Frank Lampard
P Neville: David James
Owen: David James
Terry: David James
Wright-Phillips: David James

Quiz

1. **Brazil has won the World Cup more often than any other team. How many times have they been champions?**
   a) Three
   b) Four
   c) Five
   d) Six

2. **No team has appeared in every World Cup finals but Brazil have come closest, only missing one tournament. True or false?**

3. **What links Sándor Kocsis (Hungary), Just Fontaine (France), Gerd Müller (West Germany) and Gabriel Batistuta (Argentina)?**
   a) They've each scored three own goals at World Cup finals
   b) They've each scored two hat tricks in World Cup finals
   c) They've each been sent off in two different games in one tournament
   d) They've each scored the winning goal in a World Cup final

4. **How many times has the host nation won the World Cup?**

5. **The World Cup has been held every four years since the first tournament in 1930 – true or false?**

6. **Which team have been World Cup runners-up more times than any other country?**
   a) Argentina
   b) Brazil
   c) Italy
   d) West Germany

7. In which World Cup tournament were the most goals scored?

a) Italy '90

b) USA '94

c) France '98

d) Japan and South Korea '02

8. Since the first tournament in 1930 just seven countries have won the World Cup – true or false?

9. Frenchman Abel Lafleur and Italian Silvio Gazzarriga have both had their hands on the World Cup. How?

a) They each managed World Cup winning teams

b) They were both caught trying to steal the trophy

c) They each designed a World Cup trophy

d) They are security guards hired by FIFA to accompany the trophy whenever it is put on display

10. Which football team did World Cup superstars Pelé, Bobby Moore and Ossie Ardiles all play for?

11. 1990 saw a new record for bookings in a World Cup tournament. How many yellow and red cards were dished out?

a) 112 yellows and 10 reds

b) 137 yellows and 12 reds

c) 151 yellows and 14 reds

d) 164 yellows and 16 reds

12. How many UK teams took part in the World Cup in USA?

a) 0

b) 1

c) 2

d) 3

13. Which of these teams didn't make their first World Cup finals appearance in 2002?

a) China

b) Ecuador

c) Jamaica

d) Senegal

14. Hosts Germany and 2002 World Cup winners Brazil both automatically qualified to compete in 2006. True or false?

15. The 2006 finals begin on Friday 9th June 2006. When did the World Cup final take place?

a) Saturday 1st July

b) Sunday 9th July

c) Saturday 15th July

d) Sunday 23rd July

Maze

Help Peter Crouch make his way past the defenders to score for England!

GOAL!

Wordsearch

All these countries qualified for the 2006 World Cup finals — can you find them in this wordsearch?

```
B Y P P E P S D A A G I A W A
R L O D A B O N N E E C D I H
A C R N K R A L R A I R S B R
Z P T A F H A M A R L I O F W
I E U L G B A G A N N G Y K X
L Y G R P N J T U U D A N N A
C L A E Y V S W T A N G Y E I
Q A L Z H O N R J G Y V X O T
S T Y T C O B R O D A U C E A
A I S I B I K L I R A N K W O
O N K W O G A R W K G L T O R
X L G S A R G E N T I N A A C
O C I X E M R U K R A I N E R
G B O H K Q A N S H T S O C O
U H O V J P U W F A M W J S G
```

ANGOLA	GERMANY	POLAND
ARGENTINA	GHANA	PORTUGAL
BRAZIL	IRAN	SWITZERLAND
COSTA RICA	ITALY	TUNISIA
CROATIA	KOREA	UKRAINE
ENGLAND	MEXICO	USA
ECUADOR	PARAGUAY	

Spot the Ball

Can you spot the ball in these four action shots?

Mark an X in the square you think the ball is in.

Spot the Difference

There are five differences between these two pictures of Gary Neville in action. Can you spot them all?

Design a New England Strip

Time for a change of kit! Design a new England strip to wear when you win the World Cup. You'll need a home, away and goalkeepers' strip.

ENGLAND (HOME)
ENGLAND (AWAY)

GOALKEEPER (HOME)   GOALKEEPER (AWAY)

Page 46: Quiz

1. C. Brazil were the winners in 1958, 1962, 1970, 1994 and 2002

2. It's false – Brazil have appeared in every tournament. No wonder they've won it so many times!

3. B. Kocsis and Müller scored their hat tricks in consecutive matches too!

4. Six times – Uruguay (1930), Italy (1934), England (1966), West Germany (1974), Argentina (1978) and France (1998)

5. False – there were no tournaments in 1942 and 1946 because of the Second World War

6. D. West Germany lost the final in 1966, 1982 and 1986 – Germany also lost in 2002. Argentina, Brazil and Italy have all been runners-up twice

7. C. France '98 saw a record-breaking 171 goals. Next best was Japan and South Korea with 161

8. True – Uruguay, Italy, West Germany, Brazil, England, Argentina and France are the only winners up to and including 2002

9. C. Lafleur designed the original trophy that was given to Brazil in 1970. Gazzarriga designed the trophy that is still used today

10. They all played for the Allies team in the movie Escape To Victory. Sylvester Stallone and Michael Caine were in the side too!

11. B.

12. A. It was the first time no UK team had appeared since 1950 when England became the first British team to take part in the finals.

13. C. Jamaica made their first and so far only appearance in 1998

14. It's false. A rule change meant that Brazil didn't receive a place and had to enter the qualifying tournament. Germany, however, did automatically qualify

15. B.

Page 49: Maze

Page 50: Wordsearch

Page 52: Spot The Ball

Answer: C5

Answer: D5

Answer: D1

Page 54: Spot The Ball

Answer: D3

Captain's Armband Set

Rubber ball, 500ml water bottle, mini pump, and captain's armband.

750ml Water Bottle

Plastic Shinguards

Goalkeeper Gloves

England Total Action Football

The great table top action game that recreates the excitement, pace and skill of a real International match! With magnetic action, each of the players can pass, shoot or trap the ball.

Storage Solutions

Affordable, durable storage for kids and adults alike. Light weight, collapsible and easy to clean ideal storage solutions for any England fan!

England Total Action Football available at all good toy shops. For further information, call Vivid Imaginations on 01702 200660. Bedroom items by Zap, available from all good high street stores and mail order companies including Argos, GUS, Toys R Us and Rosebys. Storage solutions by Wesco available from Shop Direct and Argos. For further information call the Wesco helpline on 0870 516 8194. Other items by Hy-Pro, available from JJB, Toys R Us, Toymaster and Woolworths or call 0870 402 1921 for your nearest stockist.